HARVEST of HEALTH

by Gloria Copeland

Harrison House
Tulsa, Oklahoma

Harvest of Health

ISBN 0-88114-841-5   KC-841-5   30-0527

©1992 Kenneth Copeland Publications

Reprinted 1998

All scripture is from the *King James Version*
unless otherwise noted.

Published by Harrison House, Inc.
P.O. Box 35035
Tulsa, Oklahoma 74153

God Wants You Well!

I have some revolutionary news for you today. God wants you healthy! Every day!

Oh, I know that, you may quickly think, *I know God will heal me when I get sick.*

Yes, that's true, He will. But that's not what I'm saying. I'm telling you God's perfect will is for you to live continually in divine health. His will is for you to walk so fully in the power of His Word that sickness and disease are literally pushed away from you. Isn't that good news?

You've probably heard a lot about God's healing power, but there is a difference between divine healing and divine health. Years ago, the powerful preacher John G. Lake put it this way, "Divine healing is the removal by the power of God of the disease that has come upon the body. But divine health is to live day by day, hour by hour in touch with God so that the life of God flows into the body just as the life of God flows into the mind or flows into the spirit."

I agree that it is wonderful to get healed when you're sick, but it's more wonderful to live in divine health. And that's what God has always intended for His people.

Even under the old covenant God promised His people immunity from disease. Exodus 23:25 says, *"And ye shall serve the Lord your God, and he shall bless thy bread, and thy water;*

and I will take sickness away from the midst of thee."

That promise is even stronger under the new covenant. Isaiah, looking forward to what Jesus would accomplish at the cross wrote, *"Surely he [Jesus] hath borne our griefs, and carried our sorrows...he was wounded for our transgressions, he was bruised for our iniquities: the chastisement of our peace was upon him; and with his stripes we are healed"* (Isaiah 53:4-5).

The Apostle Peter, looking back at that same event wrote, *"Who his own self bare our sins in his own body on the tree, that we, being dead to sins, should live unto righteousness: by whose stripes ye were healed"* (1 Peter 2:24).

Were healed! That's past tense. Jesus finished your healing on the cross. He paid the price for you to be whole. He bought righteousness for your spirit, peace for your mind, and healing for your body.

As far as Jesus is concerned, you're not the sick trying to get healed. You're the healed and Satan is trying to steal your health. I remember when Ken and I realized that, it changed everything for us. We quit trying to talk God into healing us and began instead resisting sickness and disease the way we resisted sin.

No Third Story on a Vacant Lot

Once you understand God's will really is for you to live in divine health, you can't help but question why so many believers live sick. It seems puzzling at first. But the answer is very simple. Many of them just aren't willing to do what it takes to be well.

People want to be well. No one wants to be sick. But to be well, you have to make choices. How often have you seen someone with a hacking cough still smoking a cigarette? Or an overweight person eating an ice cream cone?

Our fleshly nature likes to take the easy way. And it's much easier to give in to habits than to break them. It's easier to give in to your flesh and watch television every night like the rest of the world, than to spend your time putting God's healing Word into your heart.

I recently heard Charles Capps say that some people try to build the third story of a building on a vacant lot. That sounds funny, but spiritually speaking it's true. A lot of people want to enjoy the benefits of healing without building the foundation for it from the Word of God.

It can't be done. If you want a building, you have to start below ground level. If you want a harvest, you're going to have to plant something first.

Everything in the natural world works that way. Ken calls it the law of genesis. This law of planting and reaping works in the spirit realm too. It governs health, prosperity—in fact, everything in God's kingdom is governed by the law of planting and reaping.

Jesus taught about it in Mark 4:26-29. There, He said:

So is the kingdom of God, as if a man should cast seed into the ground; And should sleep, and rise night and day, and the seed should spring and grow up, he knoweth not how. For the earth bringeth forth fruit of herself; first the blade, then the ear,

**after that the full corn in the ear.
But when the fruit is brought
forth, immediately he putteth
in the sickle, because the harvest is come.**

According to the law of sowing and
reaping, if you want health, you need
to do more than just want it. You
even need to do more than believe in
healing. You need to plant seed that
will eventually grow up and yield a
harvest of health.

What kind of seed produces physi-
cal health? Proverbs 4:20-22 tells us:
*"My son, attend to my words; incline
thine ear unto my sayings. Let them
not depart from thine eyes; keep them
in the midst of thine heart. For they
are life unto those that find them,
and* health *to all their flesh."*

That word *health* in Hebrew
means *medicine.* God's Word has life

in it. It is actually spirit food. As you feed on it, you become strong spiritually and physically.

"Let them not depart from thine eyes." Read the Word. Meditate on the Word. That's taking God's medicine. If you will be faithful to take it continually, it eventually will be as hard for you to get sick as it ever was for you to get well.

But it's a process. You can't just read the healing scriptures once and then go on about your business. You must continually feed on the Word of God to keep the crop of healing coming up in your life.

What Did You Say?

Isaiah 55:11 says the Word of God prospers (or succeeds) in the thing for which it is sent. That means His Word about healing will produce healing. It may not produce it right away, but the more you let the Word work in you, the greater your results will be.

In other words, the size of your harvest will depend on how much seed you plant. How much time and attention you give to the Word of God will determine how much crop you will yield.

You see, your heart is actually your spirit. Its capacity is unlimited. You can plant as much seed in your heart as you have hours in a day.

If you'll build your life around the Word, you can have a full return. Jesus called it a hundredfold return (Mark 4:20).

Now some people will argue about that. They'll say, "Well, it didn't work for me! I put God's Word about healing into my heart and I'm still sick!"

But do you know what? They give themselves away the minute they say such things. Jesus taught, *"...of the abundance of the heart his mouth speaketh"* (Luke 6:45). If those people had actually planted God's Word in their hearts in abundance, they'd be talking about healing, not sickness! They would be saying, "By His stripes I am healed!"

The same is true for you. The more you put God's Word in your heart, the stronger you'll become. And eventually that Word inside you will begin to come out of your mouth in power and deliverance.

Don't wait until you have a need to start speaking the Word. Start speaking it now.

I'll never forget the first time I realized the importance of speaking God's Word. It was years ago when Ken had just started preaching and I was staying at home with our children. We were in a desperate situation financially and I was eager for answers.

One day as I was sitting at my typewriter, typing notes and listening to tapes, I read Mark 11:23. *"For verily I say unto you, That whosoever shall say unto this mountain, Be thou removed, and be thou cast into the sea; and shall not doubt in his heart, but shall believe that those things which he saith shall come to pass; he shall have whatsoever he saith."*

Suddenly, the truth of that last phrase just jumped out at me. And the Lord spoke to my heart and said, *In consistency lies the power.*

He was telling me that it's not just the words you speak when you pray that change things, it's the words you speak *all* the time!

If you want to see your desire come to pass, you need to make your words match your prayers. Don't try to pray in faith and then get up and talk in unbelief. Talk faith all the time!

Romans 4:17 says God *"...calleth those things which be not as though they were."* So if you want to receive something from God, follow His example. Speak it. That's the way faith works. You speak the Word of God concerning what you want to happen.

If what you're looking for is health, then go to the Word that tells you, "By His stripes you were healed," and put that in your mouth. Don't talk sickness. Talk health. Don't talk the problem. Talk the answer.

What You Plant Always Grows

"But Gloria," you say, "all that sounds so simple!"

It *is* simple! Sometimes I think that's why God chose me to teach it. Because I'm simple. When I read the Word of God, I just believe it is speaking to me personally. I don't worry and fuss and say, "Well, I wish that would work for me, but I don't think it will because of this or that..." I just expect God to do what He says.

You can do the same thing. You can come to the Word like a little child and say, "Lord, I receive this. I believe Your Word above all and I trust You with my life." If you will, you'll never be disappointed.

How can you get that kind of simple, childlike faith? By hearing the Word of God.

Romans 10:17 says, *"faith cometh by hearing, and hearing by the word of God."* But you need to know something else: Doubt comes by hearing also. That's why Jesus said, *"Be careful what you are hearing..."* (Mark 4:24, *The Amplified Bible*).

What you're hearing can be a matter of life and death when you're dealing with healing. If you're going to a church, for example, that teaches healing has passed away or that God uses sickness to teach you something—and you keep hearing that Sunday after Sunday— what do you think will grow in your heart? Doubt, not faith.

What you plant inside your heart grows—always. Doubt will grow and keep you bound. Truth will grow and make you free. So be careful what you're hearing. Listen to the Word of God. As Proverbs 4:21 says, *"Let them [that Word] not depart from thine eyes; keep them [it] in the midst of thine heart."*

Read the Word every day. Make note cards for yourself using the healing scriptures and tape them to your mirror.

Play teaching tapes. Listen to them in your car. Listen to them while you dress in the morning. If you'll listen to the Word while you're driving back and forth to work every day, you'll be surprised how fruitful that time will become. It will change your life. I challenge you to try it!

Don't Let Them Throw You

God's Words have power in them. When you keep them in the midst of your heart, they become life and heal-ing and health. They're medicine. God's medicine.

But beware. People will try to discourage you and keep you from taking that medicine. They'll tell you things like, "If God wants us to live in divine health, why did Sister So-and-so suffer so much sickness? And she was a fine Christian."

Don't let them throw you off track. Instead, just remember this: You don't live in divine health because you're a fine Christian. No one does. You live in divine health because you take the Word of God, and you keep it in front of your eyes. You keep it going in your ears. You keep it in the midst of your heart and you apply it to your life.

You live in divine health because you believe God for it, because you talk about it, and because you act on it—day, after day, after day.

Don't wait until an emergency comes. Don't wait until your body is weak and sick to start feeding on healing scriptures. Start now. Plant God's Word of healing in the good faith-soil of your heart daily—and then, get excited. Your harvest of health is on its way!

Prayer for Salvation and Baptism in the Holy Spirit

Heavenly Father, I come to You in the Name of Jesus. Your Word says, *"...whosoever shall call on the name of the Lord shall be saved"* (Acts 2:21). I am calling on You. I pray and ask Jesus to come into my heart and be Lord over my life according to Romans 10:9-10. *"If thou shalt confess with thy mouth the Lord Jesus, and shalt believe in thine heart that God hath raised him from the dead, thou shalt be saved."* I do that now. I confess that Jesus is Lord, and I believe in my heart that God raised Him from the dead.

I am now reborn! I am a Christian—a child of Almighty God! I am saved! You also said in Your Word, *"If ye then, being evil, know how to give good gifts unto your children: HOW MUCH MORE shall your heavenly Father give the Holy Spirit to them that ask him?"*

(Luke 11:13). I'm also asking You to fill me with the Holy Spirit. Holy Spirit, rise up within me as I praise God. I fully expect to speak with other tongues as You give me the utterance (Acts 2:4).

Begin to praise God for filling you with the Holy Spirit. Speak those words and syllables you receive—not in your own language, but the language given to you by the Holy Spirit. You have to use your own voice. God will not force you to speak.

Now you are a Spirit-filled believer. Continue with the blessing God has given you and pray in tongues each day. You'll never be the same!

Find a good Word of God preaching church, and become a part of a church family who will love and care for you as you love and care for them.

We need to be hooked up to each other. It increases our strength in God. It's God's plan for us.

Books by Kenneth Copeland

* A Ceremony of Marriage
  A Matter of Choice
  Covenant of Blood
  Faith and Patience—The Power Twins
* Freedom From Fear
  From Faith to Faith—A Daily Guide to Victory
  Giving and Receiving
  Healing Promises
  Honor Walking in Honesty, Truth & Integrity
  How to Conquer Strife
  How to Discipline Your Flesh
  How to Receive Communion
  Love Never Fails
* Now Are We in Christ Jesus
* Our Covenant With God
* Prayer—Your Foundation for Success
  Prosperity Promises
  Prosperity: The Choice Is Yours
  Rumors of War
* Sensitivity of Heart
  Six Steps to Excellence in Ministry
  Sorrow Not! Winning Over Grief and Sorrow
* The Decision Is Yours
* The Force of Faith
* The Force of Righteousness
  The Image of God in You
  The Laws of Prosperity
* The Mercy of God
  The Miraculous Realm of God's Love
  The Outpouring of the Spirit—The Result of Prayer
  The Power of the Tongue
  The Power to Be Forever Free
  The Troublemaker
  The Winning Attitude
* Welcome to the Family
* You Are Healed!
  Your Right-Standing With God

*Available in Spanish

Books by Gloria Copeland

* And Jesus Healed Them All
  Are You Ready?
  Build Yourself an Ark
  From Faith to Faith—A Daily Guide to Victory
  God's Success Formula
* God's Will for You
  God's Will for Your Healing
  God's Will Is Prosperity
  God's Will Is the Holy Spirit
  Harvest of Health
  Healing Promises
  Love—The Secret to Your Success
  No Deposit—No Return
  Pressing In—It's Worth It All
  The Power to Live a New Life
  The Unbeatable Spirit of Faith
* Walk in the Spirit
  Walk With God
  Well Worth the Wait

*Available in Spanish

Other Books Published by KCP

Heirs Together by Mac Hammond
John G. Lake—His Life, His Sermons,
  His Boldness of Faith
Winning the World by Mac Hammond

World Offices
of Kenneth Copeland Ministries

For more information about KCM and a
free catalog, please write the office nearest you:

Kenneth Copeland Ministries
Fort Worth, Texas 76192-0001

Kenneth Copeland
Locked Bag 2600
Mansfield Delivery Centre
QUEENSLAND 4122
AUSTRALIA

Kenneth Copeland
Private Bag X 909
FOUNTAINEBLEAU
2032
REPUBLIC OF SOUTH AFRICA

Kenneth Copeland
Post Office Box 15
BATH
BA1 1GD
ENGLAND

Kenneth Copeland
Post Office Box 378
Surrey
BRITISH COLUMBIA
V3T 5B6
CANADA

UKRAINE
L'VIV 290000
Post Office Box 84
Kenneth Copeland Ministries
L'VIV 290000
UKRAINE